GERMAN PARATROOPS IN THE MED

See page 26.

BRUCE QUARRIE

GERMAN PARATROOPS IN THE MED

WORLD
WAR
2
PHOTO
ALBUM
NUMBER 7

A selection of German wartime photographs
from the Bundesarchiv, Koblenz

PSL Patrick Stephens, Cambridge

First published in 1979

British Library Cataloguing in Publication Data
German paratroops in the Mediterranean. –
(World War 2 photo album; 7).
1. Germany. Heer – Parachute
troops – Pictorial works
2. World War, 1939–1945 – Campaigns
– Mediterranean region – Pictorial works
I. Quarrie, Bruce   II. Bundesarchiv
III. Series
940.54'21   D757.63

ISBN 0 85059 345 X (Casebound)
ISBN 0 85059 336 O (Softbound)

Design by Bob Swan

Photoset in 10pt Plantin Roman. Printed in Great
Britain on 100 gsm Pedigree coated cartridge and
bound by The Garden City Press Limited,
Letchworth, Hertfordshire SG6 1JS, for the pub-
lishers, Patrick Stephens Limited, Bar Hill,
Cambridge, CB3 8EL.

CONTENTS

Acknowledgements
The author and publisher would like to express their sincere thanks to Dr Matthias Haupt and Herr Meinrad Nilges of the Bundesarchiv for their assistance, without which this book would have been impossible.

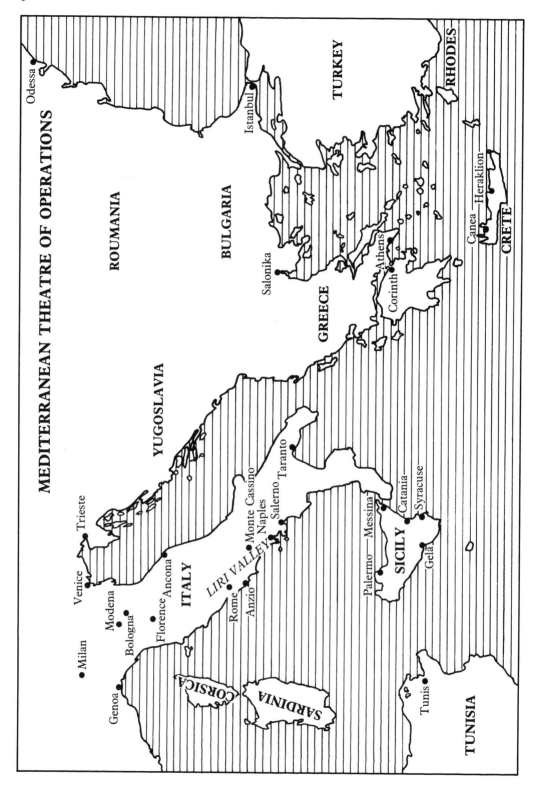

MEDITERRANEAN THEATRE OF OPERATIONS

The time: 0500 hours on April 26 1941. The place: Larissa, a town on the Thessalian plain of Greece. German paratroop forces were about to administer a severe shock to the Empire Expeditionary Force under the British General Wilson. Greek forces in the north had already surrendered to the Germans and Wilson had decided to evacuate his troops into the Peloponnese. Their only route lay across the narrow neck of land west of Athens divided by the Corinth Canal. But General Kurt Student's paratroopers were determined to get there first to seize and hold the one and only bridge, trapping the Empire troops between the sea and the German forces pressing down from the north.

The operation was almost as great a success as the capture of the Belgian fortress of Eben Emael had been the previous summer. Two battalions of the 2nd Fallschirmjäger Regiment, supported by engineers, an artillery battery, medical and signals units, dropped on both sides of the canal. The guards on the bridge were taken by surprise, and the German engineers began removal of the demolition charges on the bridge. Unfortunately, a stray shell set them off and the bridge was destroyed.

Nevertheless, the paratroopers succeeded in establishing bridge-heads on both sides of the canal, captured Corinth airfield, and held out until advance elements of the main German Army reached them 12 days later. For the Fallschirmjäger, their first Mediterranean operation had been a success although it was subsequently established that they had jumped two days late, and the bulk of the Commonwealth forces in Greece had succeeded in escaping by sea to Crete.

Formation of a German paratroop force had begun in October 1935 from elements of the 'General Göring' Regiment (for further details see my Osprey/Vanguard book *Fallschirmpanzerdivision 'Hermann Göring'*).

However, the force did not amount to a great deal until after July 1938, when Luftwaffe General Kurt Student became GOC. By the outbreak of war there were two Fallschirmjäger Regiments in existence, together with a variety of supporting troops. They fought bravely in the Polish and Norwegian campaigns, but their capture of the Eben Emael fortress – key to the Albert Canal – in 1940 was the exploit which first brought them really into the public eye. Yet greater things were still to come.

After the fall of Greece, General Student and others proposed to Hitler that the victory was only half complete since Crete still remained firmly in British hands, and this unsinkable aircraft carrier put the vital Rumanian oilfields within reach of British bombers. It was also suggested that such an operation could be conducted with relative impunity because the Allied forces, having lost Greece, were bound to be demoralised. Nothing could have been further from the truth! The tough Australian, British and New Zealand troops under the command of General Freyberg were established in strong positions and were just waiting for the Germans to try something. Far from being a surprise operation against demoralised opponents, the paratroopers were to encounter a co-ordinated and stubborn resistance.

The first wave of troops was shot to pieces. They had been divided into three groups and given the targets of Maleme airfield; Chania, Souda Bay, and Rethymno airfield; and the city and airfield of Heraklion. Unfortunately, many units became split up on landing, others fell right in the middle of Allied positions, and the remainder encountered stiff resistance which prevented their taking their prime objectives. By noon on the day of the drop – May 20 1941 – only two out of three battalions were still combat effective. However, the German High Command in Athens did not know this. All they knew was that losses among the Junkers Ju 52 transport aircraft had been very light, and orders were given to hasten their turn-around with the second assault wave of two regiments.

Unfortunately, the aircraft had to be refuelled by hand from cans, and great clouds of dust over the airfields prevented a co-ordinated take-off. The Ju 52s of the second wave thus arrived over Crete in small groups rather than as a concerted force. And, of course, the thoroughly alerted Empire troops were waiting for them.

Many of the paratroopers dropped in the wrong places and were destroyed in detail. Those landing at Heraklion ran into unexpected resistance from British tanks, and many men were mown down as they struggled to extricate themselves from their parachute harnesses. At Maleme things were a little brighter since the Germans had succeeded in capturing the important high ground overlooking the field despite all the efforts of the stubborn New Zealand defenders. Student now made the correct decision – concentrate everything on Maleme and establish a secure bridge-head. Colonel Ramcke was sent to take over from General Meindl, who had been wounded. He went in on May 21 and by early evening of that day the airfield, town of Maleme and surrounding area were firmly in German hands. Now the Ju 52s had somewhere to land, and the position was rapidly reinforced with mountain troops (Gebirgsjäger). An Allied counter-attack during the night of May 21/22 was repulsed and by the time Generalmajor Ringel, commander of the 5th Gebirgsjäger Division, arrived to take command, the bulk of his 85th and 100th Regiments were firmly entrenched against the intermittent artillery bombardment.

An amphibious assault designed to support the airborne invasion met with near disaster. One of the two flotillas of light craft – mainly captured Greek coasters and fishing boats – ran into a British Naval squadron of cruisers and destroyers and was decimated. The second squadron almost suffered in identical fashion and only managed to land safely due to the valiant action of an Italian MTB. Revenge was nigh, however, because the Luftwaffe caught up with the British Naval squadron and attacked in force, sinking a destroyer and two cruisers and damaging other vessels.

Once ashore, General Ringel ordered a two-pronged attack on the Souda Bay capital of Chania, one an outflanking move southeast through the mountains to turn the New Zealanders' flank, the other a frontal pinning operation. Both were successful, the New Zealand defences were broken on May 26 and Chania fell to the Germans on the 27th. Around 10,000 Empire troops were captured. Freyberg, realising the game was up, ordered evacuation and, while a fierce rearguard action was fought against the 100th Gebirgsjäger Regiment, succeeded in evacuating some 17,000 troops by sea to Egypt.

Losses on both sides had been high due to the fierceness of the fighting. In addition to the 10,000 mentioned, the Allies lost approximately a further 6,000 killed, captured and wounded. However, German losses from the total attack force of 22,000 had also been high – 3,250 dead or missing and 3,400 wounded. The number of missing was exceptionally high, and is usually attributed to Cretan partisans taking a hand – for which there were to be later reprisals.

The survivors returned to Germany as heroes. Parading through their garrison towns they were greeted by exultantly cheering crowds and garlands of flowers. One of the most audacious operations of the war was over. But it had its repercussions. Hitler decreed that airborne operations were too costly, and henceforward the élite paratroopers were to fight predominantly as infantry.

Fallschirmjäger operations in Russia are outside the scope of this volume, so we must now turn to North Africa. Following the Cretan operation, the paratroop forces were rapidly expanded and an intensive training programme instituted in Italy by Ramcke, now a General. The next target – Malta. However, Operation 'Herkules', conceived as a joint German–Italian airborne and naval venture, was not to be. Rommel's offensive of May 1942 appeared to be sweeping all before it, Tobruk finally fell, and the Nile delta seemed to be just a stone's throw away. Convinced that the British Navy would now concentrate at Malta, and certain that the Italian Fleet would run rather than give battle, Hitler called the operation off. Student and Ramcke were stunned. The Luftwaffe had total aerial superiority over Malta, they argued, and the British Navy would not be allowed to intervene. But Hitler was adamant and Operation 'Herkules' fell into the limbo of military might-have-beens.

Ramcke's Fallschirmjäger Brigade which had been training for the Malta operation was now despatched to North Africa, to reinforce Rommel's troops who had run out of steam at El Alamein. For two months they fought in the front line at this obscure desert railway station. They missed Montgomery's hammer blow on October 23 which fell in the north, but within a few days, together with the other German units in the south of the position, were in severe danger of being cut off. On November 2 Ramcke was ordered to withdraw.

Unfortunately, apart from the anti-tank and artillery units, the Brigade was unmotorised and, short of food, water and ammunition, the paratroopers had to slog it by foot west and north towards the coast road. However, a stroke of luck came at dawn on November 6 when, despairing of rejoining the main German force, the Brigade ran across a British truck convoy. Falling on it with glee, they soon overwhelmed the unfortunate British force and captured the trucks virtually intact! The following day they made contact with Rommel's main force after a fantastic 220-mile trek across the desert wastes. Brigade commander Ramcke earned Oak Leaves to accompany his Knight's Cross after this operation.

After Alamein, however, and more especially after the Anglo-American amphibious invasion of Morocco in November 1942, the Axis cause in North Africa was really lost. Despite being reinforced by the 5th Fallschirmjäger Regiment, there was little the courageous German paras could do to stem the tide of Allied victory. The German troops in the theatre received too little help too late – even the presence of some of the first Tiger tanks to be encountered by the Allies being of only minimal significance – and the end was a foregone conclusion.

Foregone though it may have been, the German forces continued to inflict painful losses on the Allies – particularly the 'green' American troops. The paras fought hard in Tunisia under overall command of von Arnim's 5th Panzer Army, but were finally overwhelmed in defensive operations against the British 1st Army outside Tunis in May 1943. The majority entered captivity.

Apart from those troops already serving in Russia, the balance of the German airborne forces at this time were held in reserve in southern France. Their turn for action came in July 1943 when Allied troops invaded the island of Sicily at the toe of Italy. The 3rd Parachute Regiment, commanded by Colonel-Leutnant Heilmann, jumped in the Catania area on the 12th where, a couple of days later, they were reinforced by machine-gun, artillery, anti-tank and engineer units and thrown into the front line. They came under command of the 'Hermann Göring' Division's Group 'Schmalz'.

The 3rd Regiment had a narrow escape on July 14 when it was cut off by British commandos and the 1st Airborne Brigade which landed behind it on the plain of Catania, capturing the Simeto bridge. Under dead of night, the regiment's personnel sneaked quietly in single file under the bridge and away, regaining contact with the main German force on the 16th.

The Fallschirmjäger were in the forefront of the remainder of the Sicilian fighting; despite their positions being betrayed to the Allies by the Mafia – who were extracting huge amounts of loot through re-directing food, clothing and matériel – they succeeded in holding valiantly on to the ridges on the southern flank of the German position during the withdrawal upon Messina. Elements of the 3rd Fallschirmjäger Regiment were, it is said, the last German troops to be evacuated across the Straits to mainland Italy.

Here, they were initially stationed in Calabria and around Apulia but, after barely a fortnight's respite, the battle was joined again when Montgomery's 8th Army began pouring ashore on September 3. In the intervening period the Americans had landed at Salerno – the Mussolini régime having collapsed at the end of July – and German defences were stretched to the limit. Despite a murderous beach-head response which the Anglo-Americans had not anticipated sufficiently, by this time they were pouring ashore in such numbers that the overstretched 16th Panzer Division was at the point of collapse. A battalion of the 3rd Fallschirmjäger Regiment was detached in support and, after a forced march, succeeded in a single day in restoring a degree of equilibrium to the front as well as taking more than four times their own number of British soldiers prisoner.

But the story was the same as elsewhere; the Reich was over-extended; the Allies had numerical and material superiority and, without transferring further divisions from Russia (a cure worse than the disease), the Salerno front was doomed to fall. That it lasted as long as September 17 is testimony to the courage of the German defenders.

By this time the Italians' hearts were not in the war. Badoglio had taken over from Mussolini on July 25 and very few Italian troops remained true to the Fascist cause. Five divisions of renegades had been assembled to hold Rome against their former allies.

Kurt Student, overall commander of

German paratroop forces, utilised his 2nd and 3rd Divisions against these troops; broke through with relatively little loss of life and forced the Italian Royal Family to flee. Similarly, German paras landed and overwhelmed the Italian Army HQ just outside Rome. Thanks to the Fallschirmjäger, the southern part of Italy had been secured for the Axis . . . for the time being.

An odd interlude at this time was the rescue of Mussolini himself from his incarceration in a hotel on the 10,000-foot Gran Sasso by a company of the Fallschirmjäger-Lehr-Bataillon. Masterminded under Hitler's direction by SS-Hauptsturmführer Otto Skorzeny after several weeks of searching for Il Duce, the glider-borne operation was a success. The Italian 'guards' offered no resistance and Mussolini – for what that was worth – was soon freed to join his Führer in Rastenburg.

Another sideshow at this time was the capture of the island of Elba from pro-Badoglio forces by the 2nd Battalion of the 7th Fallschirmjäger Regiment. The unfortunate Italians were in a hell of a mess, with very divided loyalties, at this stage of the war; but even so, the capture of 10,000 prisoners by a single battalion must say *something* for the respective fighting abilities of German and Italian troops?

But the Allies were still making progress, and had occupied the important islands of Kos, Leros and Samos (in the Aegean). Kos was recaptured by the Germans at the beginning of October, and Fallschirmjäger played a significant role in the similar recapture of Leros the following month. Samos was not retaken, however, for events elsewhere provided sufficient distraction. The centre of these will long live in the annals of military valour, regardless of the side you choose: Cassino.

Cassino was a crucial fixture in the so-called 'Gustav Line', Field Marshal Kesselring's southernmost defensive position in Italy. Cassino was – and still is – a Benedictine monastery of huge proportions built on a high hill dominating the River Liri valley – a key avenue to the magical goal: Rome. It contained, amongst other things, many precious religious relics and invaluable works of art. Before battle commenced, these were rescued by a Viennese officer of the 'Hermann Göring' Division . . . who later required the intervention of no less a person than Field Marshal Alexander to free him

from Allied imprisonment on 'looting' charges!

The battle for Cassino is usually divided for convenience into three phases: January 17 to February 18, March 15 to March 22 and May 11 to May 17 1944. During the first phase the 1st Fallschirmjäger Regiment, together with the 1st Fallschirm-MG-Bataillon and the 3rd Bataillon of the 3rd Regiment were attached to the tough 90th Panzer-Grenadier Division under General Baade, which was assigned the defence of Cassino village, the monastery and adjoining high ground.

The initial American attack on the positions centred on the tactically important high ground known as Calvary Hill, which repeatedly changed hands during a fierce battle lasting several days until it was finally secured by Captain Kratzert's 3rd Fallschirmjäger Bataillon. Undeterred, General Mark Clark renewed his offensive using two full divisions, but again they were bloodily repulsed. General Freyberg, in charge of the reserve New Zealand Corps, now initiated the momentous decision to bomb the monastery. This happened on February 15, and on the 17th Freyberg attacked with elements of 4th Indian and 2nd New Zealand Divisions. However, the bombing of the monastery had actually strengthened the German defensive positions, and once more the attacks were beaten off.

At the end of this phase of the battle events elsewhere took a significant turn when General Lucas' VI Corps landed at Anzio – north of the Cassino position, between the Gustav Line and Rome. Fortunately for the Germans, Lucas was a cautious commander who did not pursue his objective with sufficient determination, allowing the Germans time to reinforce their units in the area and build a solid defensive ring around the beach-head.

At Cassino, meanwhile, the 90th Panzer-Grenadier Division had been withdrawn and defence of these vital positions entrusted to General-Major Heidrich's 1st Fallschirmjäger Division. Against them the Allies had ranged the might of Freyberg's Empire troops and the US II Corps with vast artillery and aerial support.

On March 15 a massive air raid transformed the town of Cassino itself into rubble, killing over two-thirds of the Fallschirmjäger battalion positioned there. However, the tactical error of the bombing now revealed itself, the remaining 80 German defenders managing to hold off the New Zealanders, whose tanks were unable to deploy in the ruins.

The troops were well matched in fighting quality, however, and a singularly bloody hand-to-hand battle developed in the town ruins, especially after Ghurkas from 4th Indian Division were also thrown into the attack. These troops, indeed, almost succeeded in cutting the defenders in the town off from those in the monastery, and might have done so had not a spoiling attack by a Fallschirmjäger battalion thrown them back. By the end of the second phase of the battle for Cassino, Empire troops were in possession of most of the town, but the half-dozen depleted Fallschirmjäger battalions still held the key points, having inflicted some 3,000 casualties on 4th Indian Division alone.

The battle now entered its third phase. After a brief rest, 1st Fallschirmjäger Division was back in the front line. The German troops in this sector totalled five under-strength divisions compared with the Allies' 16. Calvary Hill was once more the focus of the first attack, this time by the Polish II Corps. At first it went well, and the single paratroop company defending the position was overrun; but a battalion-level counter-attack recaptured it for the Fallschirmjäger. How much longer could they hold out against such odds? Luckily, the question was not put to the test for, in the intervening period, the southern flank of the Cassino position had been broken by General Juin's Free French and 1st Fallschirmjäger Division was threatened with encirclement. Wisely, Field Marshal Kesselring ordered their withdrawal.

It came just in time, for the Anzio stalemate was about to be broken by the vigorous General Truscott, who had replaced Lucas. By June 4 the Allies were in the heart of Rome, despite the efforts of the paratroops fighting a strong rearguard action. The Germans fell back steadily during the summer towards the defensive positions they had established in the mountains north of Florence – the well-known Gothic Line. Here, 1st Fallschirmjäger Division was assigned the task of covering the important road from Florence to Bologna, through the Futa Pass. Here the division was once more faced with the American 5th Army, while the British

8th Army attacked on the eastern flank of the position, along the coast.

The Americans did not have an easy time of the battle, as the Fallschirmjäger were well dug-in and had the advantage of high ground. By September, however, the German defences were beginning to crumble and, despite every effort on their part to prevent breakthrough, and despite heavy rains which impeded the Allied advance, they were soon through into the wide and fertile northern Italian plain. To all intents and purposes, the war in Italy had been lost once the Gothic Line was breached. In the intervening period, of course, the Allies had also landed in France on D-Day (see No 5 in this series) and the Russians were pushing hard for Berlin. Fallschirmjäger continued to fight in north-west Europe and the east, but their Mediterranean war was over.

It is hard to account for the fighting spirit prevalent amongst most German paratroop units. After Crete they fought predominantly in a pure infantry role, their last airborne operation (during the Battle of the Bulge) coming to naught. Moreover, their ranks were increasingly swollen by recruits who had not gone through the same rigorous training of the early war years. Perhaps merely feeling part of such an élite formation has the desired effect?

German paratroop equipment was largely identical to that issued to other Wehrmacht and Luftwaffe field personnel, as described elsewhere in this series, but a few special items deserve individual mention. The FG 42 (Fallschirmjäger Gewehr 42) was a special lightweight automatic rifle which saw limited use. Weighing only $10\frac{3}{4}$ lb fully loaded, it fired standard German 7·92 mm ammunition from 20-round magazines.

A greater problem than small-arms in airborne operations was the provision of heavier support weapons, and the Germans devised a five-parachute pack for dropping artillery pieces from the air. These ranged from the little Swiss 20 mm Solothurn, which was scarcely more effective than an anti-tank rifle, through the tapered bore 2·8 cm PzB 41 to the two best-known weapons, the 7·5 cm and 10·5 cm LG 40 recoilless airborne guns. Specifically designed for Fallschirmjäger operations, these weapons were designed on special lightweight chassis utilising many hollow tubular and aluminium components. Special ammunition, which fired a blank charge backwards through a venturi to counter the recoil of the main charge, was developed in both high explosive and armour-piercing (hollow charge) forms. Each of these guns had an effective anti-tank range of around 1,500 to 1,600 yards and an effective HE range of 6,000–8,000 yards.

Other special equipment used by the Fallschirmjäger included the SdKfz 2 'Kettenrad' motorcycle tractor, a versatile little vehicle with excellent cross-country and load-carrying or towing characteristics which gave the Fallschirmjäger their badly needed ground mobility. Driven by a 4-cylinder Opel petrol engine developing 37 hp, it could travel at 45 mph with a range of 100 to 150 miles.

Naturally, in their pure infantry role, the Fallschirmjäger forces used a much wider variety of conventional vehicles and weapons, including armoured cars, half-tracks and self-propelled guns.

Fallschirmjäger dress was the everyday Luftwaffe service uniform in blue-grey material with leather jump boots and golden yellow waffenfarbe. However, Fallschirmjäger combat dress was completely different to that of other Luftwaffe field units. Headgear was a heavily padded, rimless helmet with two straps, to which a camouflaged cover could be attached. In addition, a special jump smock was worn. This came in two basic versions. The early type, as used in the 1940 operations and to some extent later until at least 1943, was tailored in grey-green cotton drill material with short legs. It was worn over the ordinary uniform and, indeed, over the personal equipment during a drop. The more common smock was tailored in splinter camouflage material and, instead of having 'legs', had skirts which could be fastened between the legs by means of press studs during a jump. Rank insignia on these smocks took the form of bars and wings worn on the upper left sleeve.

A special pair of jump trousers was also available, but ordinary blue-grey trousers appear to have been more common.

Later in the war, when the Fallschirmjäger were increasingly serving as straightforward infantry, a camouflage smock was introduced. This was three-quarter length and resembled the jump smocks, but was not intended for this purpose.

Fallschirmjäger personal equipment was identical to Wehrmacht issue with the exception of an extra bandolier of ammunition which was often worn around the neck.

In tropical conditions the German paras wore Luftwaffe lightweight sandy yellow tunic and trousers, the former having four large patch pockets, together with sidecap or peaked field cap. In Alpine conditions, lightweight white camouflage smocks could be worn over the jump smock.

A special 'Kreta' cuff title was worn by those Fallschirmjäger who had taken part in this operation.

ABOUT THE PHOTOGRAPHS

The photographs in this book have been selected with care from the Bundesarchiv, Koblenz (the approximate German equivalent of the US National Archives or the British Public Records Office). Particular attention has been devoted to choosing photographs which will be fresh to the majority of readers, although it is inevitable that one or two may be familiar. Other than this, the author's prime concern has been to choose good-quality photographs which illustrate the type of detail that enthusiasts and modellers require. In certain instances quality has, to a degree, been sacrificed in order to include a particularly interesting photograph. For the most part, however, the quality speaks for itself.

The Bundesarchiv files hold some one million black and white negatives of Wehrmacht and Luftwaffe subjects, including 150,000 on the Kriegsmarine, some 20,000 glass negatives from the inter-war period and several hundred colour photographs. Sheer numbers is one of the problems which makes the compilation of a book such as this difficult. Other difficulties include the fact that, in the vast majority of cases, the negatives have not been printed so the researcher is forced to look through box after box of 35 mm contact strips – some 250 boxes containing an average of over 5,000 pictures each, plus folders containing a further 115,000 contact prints of the Waffen-SS; moreover, cataloguing and indexing the negatives is neither an easy nor a short task, with the result that, at the present time, Luftwaffe and Wehrmacht subjects as well as entirely separate theatres of operations are intermingled in the same files.

There is a simple explanation for this confusion. The Bundesarchiv photographs were taken by war correspondents attached to German military units, and the negatives were originally stored in the Reich Propaganda Ministry in Berlin. Towards the close of World War 2, all the photographs – then numbering some $3\frac{1}{2}$ million – were ordered to be destroyed. One man in the Ministry, a Herr Evers, realised that they should be preserved for posterity and, acting entirely unofficially and on his own initiative, commandeered the first available suitable transport – two refrigerated fish trucks – loaded the negatives into them, and set out for safety. Unfortunately, one of the trucks disappeared en route and, to this day, nobody knows what happened to it. The remainder were captured by the Americans and shipped to Washington, where they remained for 20 years before the majority were returned to the government of West Germany. A large number, however, still reside in Washington. Thus the Bundesarchiv files are incomplete, with infuriating gaps for any researcher. Specifically, they end in the autumn of 1944, after Arnhem, and thus record none of the drama of the closing months of the war.

The photographs are currently housed in a modern office block in Koblenz, overlooking the River Mosel. The priceless negatives are stored in the basement, and there are strict security checks on anyone seeking admission to the Bildarchiv (Photo Archive.) Regretably, and the author has been asked to stress this point, the archives are *only open to bona fide authors and publishers, and prints can only be supplied for reproduction in a book or magazine.* They CANNOT be supplied to private collectors or enthusiasts for personal use, so *please* – don't write to the Bundesarchiv or the publishers of this book asking for copy prints, because they cannot be provided. The well-equipped photo laboratory at the Bundesarchiv is only capable of handling some 80 to 100 prints per day because each is printed individually under strictly controlled conditions – another reason for the fine quality of the photographs but also a contributory factor in the above legislation.

THE PHOTOGRAPHS

Left One of the most daring and imaginative Fallschirmjäger exploits of the war was the rescue of Mussolini from Gran Sasso (see also pages 78, 79). Here a paratrooper armed with the lightweight 7.92 mm Fallschirmjäger Gewehr 42 automatic rifle poses in front of one of the DFS 230 gliders which transported Skorzeny's assault force (567/1503A/1).

This page Packing parachutes. This was done with great care and strictly according to the manual. Packers normally worked in pairs, one acting as a check on the other for additional safety (LOC 1292, 547/682/10 and 35).

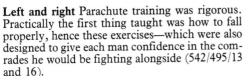

Left and right Parachute training was rigorous. Practically the first thing taught was how to fall properly, hence these exercises—which were also designed to give each man confidence in the comrades he would be fighting alongside (542/495/13 and 16).

Above far left and above left Further training took place inside converted aircraft hangars. These exercises taught recruits how to handle their lines correctly, how to steer their parachutes, and how to land safely (LOC 1288 and 547/683/33).

Above and above right Basic Fallschirmjäger equipment. This man is wearing the paratrooper helmet with double chin straps, early version smock with legs, conventional Luftwaffe trousers and jump boots. He clasps the ripcord (which would normally be attached to a static line) firmly in his left hand (78/68/5A and 78/71/5).

This page Finally the great day came and the recruits would make their first proper jump. Here they are being inspected by a training officer prior to boarding their aircraft—probably a Junkers Ju 52. Note helmet liners clearly visible in those on the ground and knee pads worn by three men for extra protection on landing (542/484/17 and 544/593/12).

Above right A recruit nervously watches the ground far below as he prepares to launch himself from a Ju 52. Note extended flaps to reduce the aircraft's airspeed (542/494/37).

Above far right and right The great moment arrives, and recruits hurl themselves into space. The ripcords are attached to static lines so that the parachutes open automatically without the recruit having to worry about anything other than the hollow feeling in his stomach. Interestingly these men appear to be jumping bareheaded (LOC 1281 and 1285).

This page The Junkers Ju 52 was the Luftwaffe's workhorse in more ways than one. This example from an unidentified unit carries a nose emblem depicting a winged angel carrying a pair of suitcases (536/125/17 and 536/123/28).

Right, inset Braced to jump. A Fallschirmjäger instructor with the rank badge of a Feldwebel demonstrates the correct method of exiting from a Ju 52. He is wearing the later pattern smock in camouflage print and without legs (584/2154/5). Background photograph The landing. Legs flexed, roll, and gather in your 'chute. Although parachutes were initially of white silk, for operational drops they were made in black or dull camouflage colours (544/593/27).

Background photograph Another widely used aircraft was the Heinkel He 111, seen here dropping 'sticks' of Fallschirmjäger (562/1171/37).

Inset View from the side machine-gunner's position of a Ju 52 (545/614/21).

Left Like the airborne forces of other nations, German para-troops did not always parachute on to their targets. The Luft-waffe made wide use of the DFS 230 glider, two of which can be seen here over a coastline (568/1528/9).

Above Towing aircraft for the DFS 230 was commonly the Junkers Ju 87 Stuka, especially after this aircraft's shortcom-ings in the dive-bomber role became revealed (567/1523/38).

Right Connecting up the towing link on the front of a DFS 230 (567/1521/23).

This page Pilot's eye view from a DFS 230 showing the Ju 87 towing aircraft and the instrument panel. What went in the empty socket I do not know (567/1521/31 and 567/1522/17).

Right and title page German paratroops demonstrate the method of exiting from DFS 230s and run into 'action' before a crowd of interested spectators. Note that several are wearing the ordinary Stahlhelm rather than the proper Fallschirmjäger helmet. Note also the MG 15 gunner perched on top of one of the fuselages (568/1529/28 and 569/1579/14).

Below right The first Fallschirmjäger operation over the Mediterranean was the drop on the Corinth Canal. The vital bridge which was later blown up can be seen at centre left. Very few pictures exist concerning this operation (LOC 798).

Background photograph The most famous airborne assault of the war, alongside Arnhem, was the attack on Crete. Unfortunately many of the units became dispersed in the air and landed in the wrong positions. This picture shows Fallschirmjäger landing near Chania on May 20 1941 (77/113/2).

Inset Aerial view of Maleme airfield after its capture (543/569/11).

This page Heavy load carrier on airborne missions was the Me 323 'Gigant' which could carry 130 troops or light armoured fighting vehicles, artillery and trucks. With a crew of five and a loaded weight of 94,815 lb, this six-engined monster could still cover 680 miles at an average speed of 136 mph (554/872/7 and 11).

Above Fallschirmjäger debouch from a DFS 230 on Crete (LOC 816).

Below Crashed Ju 52 at Maleme airfield (LOC 828).

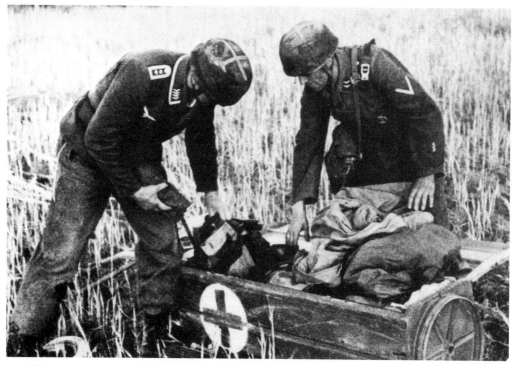

Above Unloading medical supplies from a parachute container. The man on the left has the collar insignia of an Oberfeldwebel, the one on the right that of a Gefreiter. He also has the trade badge of a medic on his lower left sleeve (LOC 865).

Above right On the ground, much use was made of local mules and donkeys as pack animals (LOC 819).

Left Artillery support was also supplied from the air. Here five parachutes support a 3.7 cm Pak anti-tank gun over Crete (LOC 853).

Right Using a stone wall for cover, a Fallschirmjäger patrol heads into the hills, probably hunting for partisans (166/508/38a).

Left Physical fitness is vital in this type of terrain, which is one reason the Fallschirmjäger were so successful (550/773/29a).

Below Pause for breath for a machine-gun section, watched by Cretan guides (550/773/32a).

Right German mountain troops (Gebirgsjäger) disembark from a Ju 52 at Maleme (LOC 826).

Below right Local handcart being used to transport supplies (570/1619/5a).

Left General Kurt Student (right) discusses the situation with General Ringel (standing) (LOC 846).

Below left General Student with a PzKpfw II on Crete (LOC 843).

Right A Fallschirmjäger private lends a hand to two wounded British prisoners (576/1842/11a).

Below General Student again (right) with Oberst Ramcke (78/68/5).

Above Medical aid for a prisoner—although I cannot understand why the paratrooper on the right appears to be stamping on his foot! (576/1829/31a).

Below Although the Empire forces fought courageously, large numbers inevitably entered captivity on Crete (576/1842/6a).

Above British and German wounded together boarding a truck (576/1827/38).

Below One thing the Germans badly lacked on Crete was transportation. Here a captured British Carrier has been impressed into their service. The men on the right appear to be Gebirgsjäger pioneers (576/1829/4a).

Above After the fighting was over—memories of a bygone age for three Luftwaffe officers (571/1702/16a).

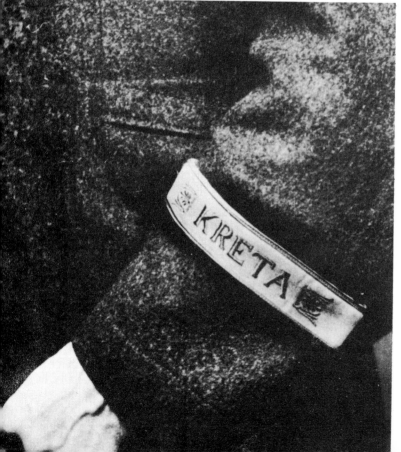

Left Close-up of the Kreta armband which was awarded to those who had taken part in the operation. Worn on the left sleeve, it was white with yellow lettering and decorative motifs. Today, such armbands are greatly sought-after collectors' items (74/168/15).

Above Next stop Africa. Here Luftwaffe personnel in greatcoats and solar topees prepare to board their Ju 52 transport (538/344/11).

Right Unloading a BMW R-75/A1 from a Ju 52 in North Africa (543/569/18).

Above Ramcke (centre) with Rommel (545/623/38).

Left Another portrait of Ramcke (548/725/28).

Above right Jacking up a Luftwaffe ambulance to replace the wheel (545/618/13).

Right The paratroops made extensive use of Italian equipment, although for the most part this was totally unsuited to 'modern' warfare. Here they have commandeered an M14/41 tank armed with a 47 mm gun. Extra armour protection has been provided by means of spare track links (546/671/17).

Background photograph Light car fitted with an anti-aircraft machine-gun. Note Ramcke Brigade insignia on mudguard and Luftwaffe number plate (556/927/24a).

Inset Fallschirmjäger personnel aboard an SdKfz 223 light armoured car. Note folding frame radio aerial (545/621/8a).

Above left Kubelwagen in Fallschirmjäger service. I have been unable to identify the unit device on the mudguard from my own references. Can any reader help? The Afrika Korps emblem and Luftwaffe number plate are, however, clearly visible (431/707/4).

Left Even in the desert, life continues as normal. The Germans allowed proxy marriages for soldiers serving overseas, and here Ramcke looks paternally on as a member of his brigade signs the documents marrying him to a girl back home (547/677/8a).

Above Oberst Barenthin (left) gives instructions to a Luftwaffe Oberleutnant (centre) and Leutnant in the desert (567/1510/32A).

Right Collar patches appear to have been worn rarely with tropical rig in the desert, as in the case of this Unteroffizier. The Luftwaffe eagle is, however, shown to advantage on both cap and tunic (548/724/30).

Above left Oberst Ramcke confers with Italian officers (546/675/22).

Left Tunisia. Fallschirmjäger personnel. The officer is wearing a 'Meyer' cap (550/754/16).

Above Ramcke Brigade motorcyclists in a Tunisian village. The insignia on the sidecar is, unfortunately, indecipherable (549/742/22).

Right Although he lacks both shoulder and collar insignia, the mapcase and binoculars suggest that this paratrooper in Tunisia is either a senior NCO or junior officer (550/754/22).

Left One of the early Tiger I tanks sent to Tunisia passes alongside a Ramcke Brigade motorcyclist (557/1018/30A).

Below left A rare picture from the Sicilian fighting. Here a British paratrooper is being interrogated by his Fallschirmjäger counterparts (550/754/21).

This page and overleaf top Fallschirmjäger in Italy. German paratroops who have been hitching a lift on an SdKfz 231 disembark to take up their positions. Note spare machine-gun barrel container carried by the man second from left in the third photo (576/1847/17a, 27 and 36).

Below left Of course, it wasn't all fighting: although the officer's rank is uncertain (his collar patches have single oak-leaves, indicating a Leutnant, Oberleutnant or Captain, but there are no 'eagles' to specify which), he appears to be doing all right for himself! (541/438/4).

Right Back in the hills, a Fallschirmjäger patrol discusses its next move (570/1610/29).

Below I don't know where this photo was taken, except that it appears to be a sunken road (or castle moat?) but it is the only picture I have so far come across of a Flak '88 crewed definitely by Fallschirmjäger as opposed to other Luftwaffe personnel (570/1614/10A).

Left An Army officer points out a direction for paratroopers in Italy; the man on the left is a Feldwebel, as can be seen from his sleeve insignia (571/1716/7a).

Above Although the Fallschirmjäger units largely lacked armoured fighting vehicles, one type that they appear to have received fairly frequently is the Marder III. Here is a heavily camouflaged example in Italy (568/1538/30A).

Below Another Marder followed by what appears to be an SdKfz 7 with armoured cab, both crewed by Fallschirmjäger, in an Italian town (570/1612/1).

Background photograph The ruins of Monte Cassino seen from an adjacent hill (579/1952/2A).
Left inset The view from Monte Cassino out over the Liri valley (74/6/62).
Right inset and following four pages Inside Cassino. This and the following ten photos clearly show the conditions existing inside Monte Cassino during and after the Allied aerial bombardment. The strain of battle is very clear on the faces of the defenders, and it is evident that in one instance a bomb or shell has landed just as the photographer was taking his picture. Note that some of the men are wearing lightweight anoraks in preference to jump smocks (577/1905/7, /1906/13, /1910/6a, /1920/16, /1923/34 and 37, 578/1926/32, 35 and 36, 578/1928/3A and 21A).

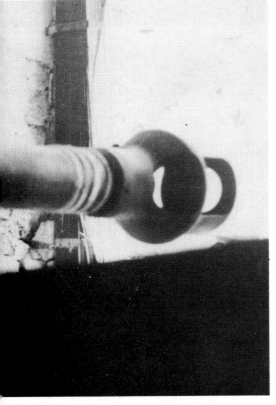

Above left Mules and donkeys were used as much on the Italian mainland as on Crete. My guess is that these two Fallschirmjäger are taking supplies to an outpost in the mountains (570/1620/17A).

Left Fallschirmjäger take shelter in an Italian ruin alongside a hastily camouflaged StuG III (567/1511/11).

This page Luftwaffe officers confer on the Nettuno front (575/1802/35 and 575/1807/31a).

Above Fallschirmjäger – two of them wearing ordinary Stahlhelms – man a 3.7 cm Pak anti-tank gun on the Nettuno front (575/1807/1a).

Below A Marder III with Fallschirmjäger crew on an Italian road. Note that one of the roadwheels has obviously been replaced by a spare from another vehicle (570/1601/8).

Right Wounded Fallschirmjäger Feldwebel in camouflage smock. Perhaps he was trying to take a photograph at the wrong time? (577/1912/24).

Far left Another Feldwebel wounded in Italy. That he is one of the survivors from the Ramcke Brigade is indicated by his 'Afrika' armband (577/1912/36).

Left Wire has been used to make a frame to hold camouflage foliage on the helmet of this para-trooper, a common practice in the German armed forces (579/1954/32A).

Right Fallschirmjäger MG 42 crew relax overlooking the ruins of an Italian village (571/1716/6a).

Below left, below and following two pages One of the weapons specially designed for airborne operations was the 10.5 cm LG 40 recoilless gun, two examples of which are being demonstrated here. The method of hitching a lift by sitting on the breech does not look very comfortable! The towing vehicle in both cases is an NSU Kettenrad half-track motorcycle. Again, I am unable to identify the unit device on the side of the Kettenrad, but the white disc as background would suggest that it could be that of a Fallschirmjäger unit within, or attached to, the 'Hermann Göring' Division (541/433/34, 543/562/22, 547/688/18, 570/1606/13, 570/1616/17A and 37A).

These pages Mortars proved especially useful in mountain warfare, with their high trajectory to carry their bombs over ridges and other obstacles. These views, which will be especially valuable to modellers, illustrate sGrW 34 8.14 cm heavy mortars in action in Italy, and also show crew poses and a variety of different clothing combinations off well (549/740/22a, 568/1539/12A, 570/1605/19 and 577/1917/8).

Above The Kettenrad (this example has lost its headlamp) was also useful for towing supplies in the small trailer shown here (570/1616/38A).

Below Wearing camouflaged jump smocks and a mixture of paratrooper and Army helmets, the crew of a 3.7 cm Pak manoeuver their gun into a firing position (579/1968/13).

Above Much more potent than the little 3.7 cm was the 5 cm Pak 38, photographed in action in Italy crewed by Fallschirmjäger personnel (569/1086/22a).

Below The 7.5 cm Pak 40 was fitted to the Marder III, seen here well camouflaged in an Italian courtyard (570/1614/22A).

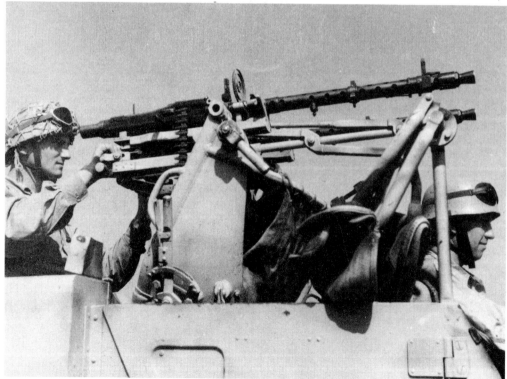

Above left As a pure infantry anti-tank weapon, the 8.8 cm RPzB 54 'bazooka' was the most effective instrument in the German inventory. Here an instructor primes a young recruit in its operation (578/1936/13A).

Left Twin MG 34 machine-guns mounted on a medium car crewed by Fallschirmjäger personnel (570/1612/28).

Above After the Italians made a separate peace, one of the less glamorous tasks which befell the Fallschirmjäger was cleaning out pockets of resistance in Rome. Here a patrol cautiously surveys the scene from a railway siding (568/1537/15).

Right Fallschirmjäger in shirt-sleeve order advance along a Roman street (570/1611/11A).

This page Fallschirmjäger anti-tank gunners with a Pak 38, believed also to have been taken in Rome during their rearguard action against the advancing Allies. Of special interest is the display card behind the gun shield showing silhouettes of a Churchill, Lee/Grant and Sherman with their more vulnerable parts marked for the gunlayer's attention (567/1515/28 and 30).

Above right A 3.7 cm Pak similarly emplaced on a street corner (570/1606/22).

Right 'O' Group discussion for Fallschirmjäger NCOs. The Obergefreiter second from right is wearing a Luftwaffe Fliegerbluse (580/1993/5).

Right inset As stated earlier (see page 15), one of the most famous Fallschirmjäger exploits was the rescue of Mussolini from his mountaintop prison. Here one of Skorzeny's DFS 230 gliders can be seen on the plateau (567/1503A/36).

Below left inset A very ill looking Mussolini (centre) with his rescuer, Otto Skorzeny, after the Gran Sasso raid (567/1503A/3).

Background photograph The view down Gran Sasso gorge with the cable car wires clearly visible (567/1503A/17).

Left Most of the work, though, was far less glamorous. Here dejected-looking Fallschirmjäger retreat along an Italian mountain road (571/1714/11a).
Below left Demonstration of an FG 42 7.92 mm automatic rifle with bipod stowed back underneath the barrel (576/1831/27a).
Right A more conventional weapon, the famous MP 40, carried here by a Fallschirmjäger Feldwebel (568/1537/38A).
Below Only here for the beer? (578/1934/19).

OVERLEAF

Background photograph For collectors of this series, an especially interesting shot as it shows a Luftwaffe war correspondent with cine camera and portable battery on his back. The foreground figure is also interesting as he is carrying an Italian Beretta modello 39A 9 mm MP 739(i) sub-machine-gun, a very popular weapon due to its excellent workmanship (585/2186/14A).
Inset An MG 42 gunner anxiously scans the skies for Allied aircraft (576/1846/13a).

Left Even supermen have to eat sometime! Fallschirmjäger with more important things on their minds than the war. The anti-aircraft gun is a 20 mm Flak-vierling 38 (582/2116/21).

Below Fallschirmjäger 'let their hair down' after a patrol. Note multiplicity of spare ammunition pouches carried by several men (566/1494/13).

Right MG 42 team keep watch from a ditch (449/762/28).

Below right Luftwaffe radio operators in the Italian sun (568/1546/26).

Left Good portrait shot of a Fallschirmjäger having just been awarded the Knight's Cross. He already has the Iron Cross both 1st and 2nd Class (539/380/15).

Below Fallschirmjäger motor-cyclists with an Italian Semovente self-propelled gun (550/774/14a).

Right Fallschirmjäger officers, suitably clad for the heat, confer. The bicycle has probably been appropriated from some unfortunate Italian villager (568/1537/25).

Above left Fallschirmjäger officers in a staff car move past a PzKpfw IVF1 in an Italian village (568/1535/26).

Left Minelaying. The Oberfeldwebel at left centre is holding a T Mi 42 – type 2 Tellermine (571/1701/23).

Above MG 42 detachment whiling the time away with records on a wind-up gramophone (570/1607/16).

Right The other side of the picture: an exhausted-looking Fallschirmjäger medical orderly (572/1743/23).

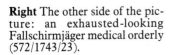

Left Field Marshal Kesselring demonstrates his ability with an MP 43 assault rifle before an interested audience of other high-ranking Luftwaffe and Wehrmacht officers (580/1980/14).

Below far left The thick lining to the Fallschirmjäger helmet is particularly clear in this portrait of an Unteroffizier (544/586/11).

Below left Fallschirmjäger sentry stands watch inside the doorway of an Italian house (570/1611/21A).

Right Come on out wherever you are: an Obergefreiter with a reel of telephone cable on his back peers into the bushes, Luger P 08 firmly in hand (541/435/30).

Below Good portrait of a young Fallschirmjäger trooper in Italy. He appears to be wearing a combat knife in some form of shoulder sheath (567/1503A/22).

Below right Despite the snow lying in patches on the hillside, these Luftwaffe personnel appear quite comfortable in the Italian sunshine. Donkeys were as useful here as on Crete (571/1705/5).

Above More suitably dressed for the cold, a paratrooper lies in wait in the Italian mountains (571/1707/25a).

Left Very posed but useful detail shot of a paratrooper in winter dress. Note whitewashed helmet (556/946/6).

Right Whither home? (571/1707/4a).

APPENDIX

Order of Battle and commanders of the 1st Fallschirmjäger Division during the second battle of Cassino, 1944

Divisional staff
CO General-Leutnant Heidrich
1a Major i.G. Heckel
1b Hauptmann i.G. Strangenberg
1c Oberleutnant Treiber

Fallschirm Signals Abteilung 1
(Hauptmann Graf)
1st Company – radio
2nd Company – field telephone

Fallschirmjäger Regiment 1
(Oberst Schulz)
Regimental staff and signals
Pioneer company
Mortar company
Anti-tank company
1st Battalion
(Major Graf v.d. Schulenburg)
Battalion staff and signals
1st, 2nd and 3rd Jäger companies
4th Machine-gun company
2nd Battalion
(Major Gröschke)
As 1st Battalion
3rd Battalion
(Major Becker)
As 1st Battalion

Fallschirmjäger Regiment 3

As 1st Regiment
1st Battalion
(Major Böhmler)

2nd Battalion
(Hauptmann Foltin)
3rd Battalion
(Major Kratzert)

Fallschirmjäger Regiment 4
(Major Grassmehl)
As 1st Regiment
1st Battalion
(Hauptmann Beyer)
2nd Battalion
(Hauptmann Hübner)
3rd Battalion
(Hauptman Meyer)

Fallschirm Artillery Regiment 1
(Major Schram)
Regimental staff and signals
1st Battalion
(Hauptmann Scheller)
1st, 2nd and 3rd batteries – 7·5 cm mountain guns
3rd Battalion
(Hauptmann Tappe)
7th, 8th and 9th batteries – 10·5 cm light guns

Fallschirm Pioneer Battalion 1
(Hauptmann Frömming)
Battalion staff and signals
1st, 2nd and 3rd Pioneer companies
4th Machine-gun company

Fallschirm Anti-tank Abteilung 1
(Major Brückner)
Abteilung staff and signals
1st, 2nd, 3rd and 4th companies – 7·5 cm Pak (towed)
5th company – 7·5 cm Pak (SP)

Fallschirm Machine-gun Battalion 1
(Major Schmidt)
Battalion staff and signals
3 Machine-gun companies

Fallschirm Medical Abteilung 1
(Oberstabsarzt Dr Eiben)
2 Medical companies

Other titles in the same series

No 1 Panzers in the desert
by Bruce Quarrie
No 2 German bombers over England
by Bruce Quarrie
No 3 Waffen-SS in Russia
by Bruce Quarrie
No 4 Fighters defending the Reich
by Bryan Philpott
No 5 Panzers in North-West Europe
by Bruce Quarrie
No 6 German fighters over the Med
by Bryan Philpott
No 8 German bombers over Russia
by Bryan Philpott

In preparation

No 9 Panzers in Russia 1941–43
by Bruce Quarrie
No 10 German fighters over England
by Bryan Philpott
No 11 U-Boats in the Atlantic
by Paul Beaver
No 12 Panzers in Russia 1943–45
by Bruce Quarrie

Plus many more!